long

a

Sounds & Letters ⑱

T0025482

KNOWLEDGE
BOOKS

lake	rake
cake	tape
rain	train
snail	

lake

3

rake

4

5

cake

tape

9

rain

11

train

13

snail

lake	rake
cake	tape
rain	train
snail	

Knowledge Books and Software
PO Box 50 Sandgate, Queensland 4017 Australia
p. +617-55680288 f. +617-55680277 email: sales@kbs.com.au

First Published 2022
ISBN 9781922516909
Text and editing: Carole Crimeen
Design and layout: Suzanne Fletcher
Publisher: Robert Watts

Series Information: **Sounds and Letters**

Credits
Photographs: Cover © wee dezign; p. 1 © Artem Kutsenko, Eric Isselee, Dionisvera, Iasha; p. 3 © ian woolcock; p. 5 © Mega Pixel; p. 7 © Africa Studio; p. 9 © Seregam; p. 11 © ND700; p. 13 © Photoongraphy; p. 15 © Aleksandar Dickov/Shutterstock.

Phonic support books are a wonderful resource for emergent readers as they encourage independent reading and help students make the link between letters and the sounds they represent.

Have students identify the images on the title page to listen for the long or short vowel sound that they will hear through the book.

Encourage students to point to each word as they read through the book.

ISBN: 9781922516909

9 781922 516909 >

KNOWLEDGE
BOOKS

Sounds&
Letters